WHI

from the

HOLLOW BONE

Wayne William Snellgrove
Fishing Lake First Nation

Aster Press
an imprint of Blue Fortune Enterprises LLC

For information contact :
Blue Fortune Enterprises, LLC
Aster Press
P.O. Box 554
Yorktown, VA 23690
http://blue-fortune.com

Cover design by Wesley Miller, WAMCreate

ISBN: 978-1-948979-51-1

First Edition: August 2021

Acknowledgements

To all my Indigenous ancestors on Turtle Island,
especially those who carried our ceremonies when the
colonial governments deemed them illegal.

Thank you for walking in a sacred way,
even though you put yourselves in harm's way so
future generations will not have to.

Introduction

THIS IS THE SECOND EDITION of this series; like the first, this book is dedicated to further deepening humanity's understanding and connection to all things powerful and beautiful both seen and unseen.

Written in simple and short but powerful truths, Spirit offers these meditations and messages to our hearts, to sit with in the ceremony of love and guidance wherever the reader chooses to be.

Let us allow the sacred to flow from the Spirit through these messages to all sacred circles, tribes, and nations. In short, let us learn to be the "hollow bones" for the rest of humanity, spearheading the beautiful 500-year awakening our indigenous ancestors prophesied.

Medicine Wheel

Also referred to as the sacred hoop, this is a physical reflection of our spiritual self. It embodies the health and the cycles of life that we live in. This aligns our spiritual life force with those around us, including Mother Earth.

Contained within the medicine wheel are the four directions and the four seasons.

EAST/
SPRING

March 20

As we approach spring, let us remember
it isn't the music that Mother Earth offers that changes
our lives, it's her music that we carry in our hearts that
changes our lives.

March 21

It is the same beautiful lifetime between
two breaths and two heart beats.
We must learn to take time and listen to both.

March 22

The sacred truth is that all our ancestors, both seen and unseen, from all nations, roads, and tribes want to be remembered, loved, and honored.

March 23

Resistance to love is Spirit's only intruder.

March 24

Everything is Medicine. Both seen and unseen.
Above and below. From Grandmother Mole to the
Stars and everything in-between.
The good, the bad, and the ugly.
It is our choice to take what we need
to live a good life.

March 25

Our prayers of love and light for others
may not change their life,
but they will always change ours.

March 26

We often tear ourselves away from the bosom of
Mother Earth and wonder why we suffer.
To be whole again, we must return
from which we came and enter into a new
continuous intimate relationship with her.

March 27

Our fears do not understand the power of courage.

March 28

The best spiritual path is praying for other spiritual
paths who do not teach praying
for other spiritual paths.

March 29

This moment can be the beginning
of anything you want.
This moment can be the end
of anything you want.

March 30

All life has a right to life.
There is no hierarchy in the words "right to life."

March 31

Every day the sun teaches us
to keep rising and try again.

April 1

All fires are direct descendants of the original fire.
The sacred fire within you is a descendant of the first
sacred fire at the center of the universe when the
universe was first created.

April 2

Our ancestors are born again when they dance their dances, sing their songs, and tell their stories. If we continue to celebrate them, they will live forever.

April 3

We are safest walking among the prayers of our
ancestors, celebrating life the way they did, offering
themselves to their ancestors before them.
We must follow what they have done before us.

April 4

Love comes in many colors, and one of the most
beautiful and most powerful of these is transparency.

April 5

We must be brave enough to follow the voice
that listens to our hearts.

April 6

Try not to get caught in yesterdays,
there are so many.
Try not to get caught up in tomorrows,
there are so many.
Try to stay in today because there is just one today.

April 7

Today, I take charge of my healing.

April 8

If the only message we are able to convey is the seed,
then that is perfect.

April 9

Our mind grows when it is open.
Our heart grows when we share it.

April 10

A new life begins when we start to remember
our dreams and our ancestors.

April 11

Life of the Flower Seed:
Seed: Just Be
Roots: Be grounded
Stem: Time to grow
Bulb: Release Beauty

April 12

Our Great Mother's wind constantly speaks to our hearts. Her gentle flowing rivers tell us stories of her love and survival. Her mountains tell us about her strength. Her vast oceans tell us about her dreams. Her moon tells us about her phases. Her fall tells us how to gracefully let go. Her winter tells how to let go of those things that no longer serve life. Her spring tells us how to gracefully accept rebirth.

April 13

Within me is all the love and courage
that my ancestors carried.

April 14

Our first inspiration from Spirit? The sunrise.
Our Second? Our breath.

April 15

Love remembers and embraces what fear forgets,
hate ignores, and ignorance rejects.

April 16

The trick is to know that we can fly
while sitting on the branch.

April 17

We are Earthlings who have lost touch with Earth.

April 18

Creator, teach me to see those things
I cannot see with my eyes.
Creator, teach me to listen to those things
I cannot hear with my ears.

April 19

Spiritual growth centers in what we want to do,
what we can do, and what we are willing to do.

April 20

Real detachment is following our own path.

April 21

Our spiritual journey begins in earnest when we
understand our relationship with all sacred circles.

April 22

The first chapter in the book of miracles is humility.
The first word in that chapter is truth.

April 23

The new world we seek is already inside our hearts.
It is found in the prayers passed down to us from
those who have come before us, our ancestors.

April 24

Beautiful things are not always perfect.
But it is always perfect when
we look for beauty in everything.

April 25

If we learn from one spiritual path,
our knowledge of the Spirit is very limited.
If we learn from many spiritual paths,
our knowledge of the Spirit is very limited.
If we learn from all spiritual paths,
our knowledge of the Spirit is very limited.

April 26

May the moonrise always remind you of your dreams.
May the sunrise always remind you of your purpose.

April 27

Good attitude or bad,
you will probably end up where you are headed.

April 28

Our spiritual goal has always been to be
a little better than we were yesterday.

April 29

Courage is a love affair with the unseen.
Faith is a love affair with the unknown.

April 30

Spring is the season that teaches us
we are brave enough to follow the voice
that listens to our hearts.

May 1

Our true power is based on our alignment with the
ancient sacred agreements of harmony and balance.

May 2

Creator, please help us,
especially when we forget to help ourselves.

May 3

Fear gives us limits the heart cannot see.

May 4

We must learn to understand the strength
Mother Earth offers. She gives it to us for free.
Strength enough for us to live in peace.
The only request she asks is that
we share her strength so the world may live in peace.
This is the way we honor her.

May 5

Enlightenment, consciousness, and awakening begins when we have pity on living things.

May 6

Willingness and courage are close relatives;
like the sun and the rain, both are necessary
for healing in a good way.

May 7

Love is how we pay our rent here on earth.

May 8

Intention is the beginning of all medicine.

May 9

Love shared is love doubled.

May 10

Let us be grateful for our last breath and hopeful for our next, and live in that moment in between.

May 11

Hollow bones is not only a ceremony but a way of life.

May 12

The Seasons tell us nothing ever dies,
it all transforms into something else.

May 13

It is the same lifetime between
two breaths and two heart beats.

May 14

We are love. Are our prayers and actions
in alignment with what we are?

May 15

Connecting to Mother Earth is understanding
she is all medicine.

May 16

Creator created love. Creator created Mother Earth.
The Medicine Mother Earth offers is love.

May 17

Just Love for the love of Loving.

May 18

The act of offering for our prayers to be heard
is the beginning of learning the power
of the sacred circle of life.

May 19

Our ability to listen to Mother Earth is based on
our connection to her.
The closer the connection,
the clearer the message.

May 20

Mother Earth doesn't *have* medicine
as much as she *is* medicine.

May 21

Spring's greatest medicine is teaching us
gentleness out of darkness is the way to growth.

May 22

Courage to overcome obstacles brings
strength to overcome the next set of obstacles.

May 23

Like the spring rains, I create as I speak.
As the water creates life, so does what we speak.

May 24

Medicine Wheel teaching:
To live a good life, adopt the nature of the seasons.

May 25

We are better people when we remember
we are part of Mother Earth
and always in ceremony.

May 26

Our mistakes are cracks where the
new beginning light sneaks in.

May 27

Mother Nature synchronizes our insides
with her outsides.

May 28

Beginning a day without prayers is like
planting a tree without roots.

May 29

The first stage of healing is to be kind and help others.
The last stage of healing is to be kind and help others.

May 30

The spiritual axiom is the closer we are to
Mother Earth, the closer we are to each other.

May 31

Love is a safe place.

June 1

When it comes to the injustices against Mother Earth,
the worst thing we can do is nothing.

June 2

Rewriting our future can be heavily influenced
by healing our attitude of the past.

June 3

Ego wants us to show up and be perfect.
Spirit wants us to show up and be better.

June 4

The Red Road begins where humility starts.
It says to follow the old ones who came before you and
to leave a trail of love for those who come after you.

June 5

Those who are awakened to the Spirit see
beauty and love before anything else.

June 6

If you only do the right thing
when someone is looking,
be mindful Spirit is always looking.

June 7

Animals understand their symbiotic, harmonious relationship with Mother Earth much more than humans ever could. We could learn much about our humanity from their looking at theirs.

June 8

That flower you are waiting to bloom is probably you.

June 9

Mother Earth is not only offering but begging for
humanity to build a better relationship with her.
Spiritually — celebrate her
Emotionally — remember her
Physically — honor her
Mentally — respect her

June 10

To make room for those tears that are yet to come,
we must learn to honor their path.

June 11

Our politics or religion do not make us a better person,
only our behavior does.

June 12

We honor our sacred path by walking it.
We defend our sacred path by walking it.

June 13

All life everywhere — the ones who fly, the ones who swim, the ones with four legs, the ones who stand — are all messengers of the Great Spirit.

June 14

Awakening humanity has always been
the spiritual revolution.

June 15

Be Grateful.
Some people dream about
what you've forgotten about.

June 16

Nothing will dim your light more than
hanging around those who do not support you.

June 17

Our Spiritual journey explained by the light:
1. See the light
2. Walk to the light
3. Become the light
4. Walk with the light
5. Share the light

June 18

Let us not confuse what we cannot do
with what we won't do because
all this talk blocks us
from what we can do.

June 19

If we teach our children to love Mother Earth
then our children will learn to love themselves.

SOUTH/
SUMMER

June 20

If helping others is below you,
then your healing is beyond you.

June 21

Medicine Wheel teaching:
All life is sacred.

June 22

It is good if we sit before flowers admiring their beauty, but if we sit before flowers learning how they bloom, that is real beauty.

June 23

The Medicine Wheel teaches us the best knowledge is
the kind that tells us to keep learning.

June 24

Humanity's only religion should be helping others.

June 25

Mother Earth has eyes and sees and hears everything. Her heartbeat lives inside us. She understands touch, has feelings and dreams. She is an extension of us, and we are an extension of her.

June 26

The Spiritual axiom is that our divine uniqueness
is what keep us the same.

June 27

Not all survivors look like superheroes,
but all superheroes like look survivors.

June 28

Hope is humanity's greatest asset.
It is only really understood by those who share it
to help plant the seed for those who receive it.

June 29

If it makes your heart dance, follow it.
If it makes your Spirit dance, dance with it.

June 30

At any one time we walk two paths:
one chasing and walking in the darkness and
one chasing and walking in the light.

July 1

The love child of hope and faith is courage.

July 2

Despite everything, love everything.
That's the only opinion that really matters.

July 3

When the truth becomes more important
than what you're running from,
healing begins.

July 4

If we want to strengthen our past,
learn from it.
If we want to strengthen our present,
carry those lessons.
If we want to strengthen our future,
teach those lessons.

July 5

Our hearts are our spiritual drum,
our direct link to Spirit and Mother Earth.
It represents the power of our unity,
the sound that connects us all.

July 6

The Heart is the keeper of the love Medicine.
Part of our spiritual journey is to find our love medicine.
After we have found it, our only way to keep it is to
honor the ancient sacred agreement to give it away.

July 7

What gives humanity the right
to forget Mother Earth?

July 8

Trying to form an educated decision
without consulting the elders is like
a flower trying to bloom without roots.

July 9

We have the same responsibility as Mother Earth:
to honor and protect all life.

July 10

Bird medicine:
A bird knows a single feather cannot help her fly.
But with many feathers working in unison,
she will understand the harmony of flight.

July 11

Failure, like the sunset, is inevitable,
but a bad attitude doesn't have to be.
A good attitude is like the sunrise.

July 12

The most beautiful and profound healing gift we give
to our ancestors is our own healing.
The most beautiful and profound healing gift
we can give to the next seven generations is
our own healing.

July 13

Loving prayers for others is
our perfect opinion of them.

July 14th

Tree Wisdom:
Just because the limbs appear to bend doesn't mean
the tree thinks it's weak or made a mistake.

July 15

It is our sacred breath that connects us all.

July 16

If we want to grow, we have to go to a place
we've never been.

July 17

Medicine Wheel teaching:
Those who only take will never be satisfied.
Those who only give will never find peace.
Those who have balance in their lives have found both.

July 18

Mother Earth reminds us we all come from
the same medicine.

July 19

As the Medicine Wheel teaches,
life is a thread that has no end.
It is an endless circle.

July 20

Our ancestors tell us our spiritual roots begin with
Mother Earth. Understanding how deeply connected
we are is the journey. The deeper we understand, the
more we know that our roots take on many forms.
They can look like the mighty mountains,
flowing rivers, a gentle breeze, the seasons
or the phases of the moon.

July 21

Love is so powerful, if it is shared anywhere
it will affect everything everywhere.

July 22

The spiritual opposite of connection is comparison.

July 23

Walk as if your feet are kissing the Earth.
Stand as if your skin is caressing the wind.
Breathe as if your breath is purifying the air.
Speak as if your words are healing
the next seven generations.
Dream as if you are protecting
the dreams of our ancestors.

July 24

The act of only taking is a practice in selfishness.
The act of only receiving leaves empty.
Together, equally, they create a balanced life.

Wayne William Snellgrove

July 25

When we decide not to give up,
we open the door for miracles.

July 26

Failure only lasts until our next breath.

July 27

We must learn to love in such a way that
the ones we love feel safe, comforted and free.
The kind of love that Mother Earth creates form us.

July 28

Perfection is the language of the ego.
Progress is the language of the heart.
Love is the language of the universe.

July 29

The real battle of the self isn't fear or hate,
it is walking in love.

July 30

Humanity will not know balance until we decide
to give Mother Earth human rights.

July 31

The supreme law of the land is found in
gentle and sacred flow.

August 1

The Sun leads.
The Moon dreams.
The Stars guide.
Mother Earth holds.

August 2

The true beauty and power of love is that
what you give away will always be a part of you.

August 3

Mistakes happen.
Be grateful you survived.
Understand you are not your mistakes.
Learn from them.
Say you're sorry.
Make amends.
Forgive yourself.
Move on.
Thank God.

August 4

Humanity's deadliest disease is not
cancer, diabetes, or heart disease,
it is our indifference to Mother Earth.

August 5

Healing comes in two disciplines:
heal now or heal later.

August 6

Not all wisdom is spoken,
nor do all messages have a voice.

August 7

Mistake are what makes us human.
Learning from them are what makes us spiritual.

August 8

When we begin to realize our oneness with all life,
every encounter becomes a divine spiritual connection.

August 9

Mother Earth has always been the leader of our tribe.

August 10

If you want to be remembered, be kind.
If you want to lift the broken, be kind.
If you want to be loved, be kind.
If you want to love, be kind.

August 11

When we educate our children to
love and appreciate Mother Earth,
we are teaching them to
connect with and love
the unseen and unheard voices.

August 12

Give the Sun your heart.
Give the Moon your secrets.
Give the Clouds your dreams.
Give the Ocean your prayers.
Give the Fire your passion.
Give the Water your tears.
Give Mother Earth your love.

August 13

Indigenous teachings:
The paradox of Indigenous Hollowbones,
Our leaders are the first ones to follow.

August 14

The seed of every fire is the original fire
at the center of the universe.

August 15

Mother Earth has a heritage and culture
that humanity is struggling to grasp.
That culture and heritage is based on her
harmony, balance, and the circle of life.

August 16

What others do, act, and say
about you doesn't define you.
How you respond to what others do, act, and say
about you is what defines you.

August 17

We act exactly, directly and according to our personal relationship with love.

August 18

We often tear ourselves away from the bosom of
Mother Earth and wonder why we suffer. To be whole
again, we must return from which we came.
Enter into a continuous, intimate relationship with her.

August 19

The breeze is the wind slow dancing.

August 20

When our intentions are pure, our tribe will find us.

August 21

Love isn't easy, and it is a challenge,
but often in life the only real challenge is to love.

August 22

It is not age nor time that will open new doors.
Only awareness. Awareness of love.

August 23

The magic that whispers in nature
sounds like the breeze through the trees.

August 24

When humanity's greed is silenced,
we will be able to hear the heart cry of Mother Earth.

August 25

The center of spirituality is in helping others.

August 26

The first step to healing Mother Earth is
realizing we are a part of her.

August 27

Forgiveness is abundance.
Healing is abundance.
Letting go is abundance.

August 28

In our hearts, we keep the sacred first flame
from the center of the universe.
A gift from the Great Spirit.
We are asked to hold this fire in a good way
for future generations.

August 29

In spiritual realms, there is a message in every moment.

August 30

We all have spiritual gifts no one else has.
Our job is to find those gifts
and share them with the world.

August 31

A lifetime of forgetting to pray for Mother Earth is relieved by one prayer for her now.

September 1

Life sometimes gives us unbearable and unfair circumstances. And we have a right to be angry, upset and terrified. But we also have a right to recover, to heal and be happy.

September 2

If we fail to lift the wounded, we fail to lift ourselves.

September 3

We do not transform into butterflies,
we transform because we are butterflies.

September 4

Often the only thing that stands in the way of our darkness is our connection to Mother Earth.

September 5

The path has always been "Love anyway."

September 6

When the beginning is near, so is the end.

September 7

When we listen to women,
we are listening to Mother Earth.
When we honor women,
we are honoring Mother Earth.
When we protect women,
we are protecting Mother Earth.

September 8

It is by offering ourselves to Spirit
that we able to help others.

September 9

Earth isn't a part of Indigenous culture,
Earth is Indigenous culture.

September 10

My religion is healing myself while helping others.

September 11

The wind does not ask the Creator if it can blow.
The stream does not ask the oak tree if it can flow.
Great things do not have to ask to be great.
Beautiful things do not have to ask to be beautiful.
And you do not have to ask to be great or beautiful,
just know that you already are.

September 12

Understanding the Red Road is knowing
that the Mother Earth has a sacred voice.
Walking the Red Road is listening to her sacred voice.
Helping others is living the Red Road.

September 13

Our willingness to connect to all life is our Spiritual job.

September 14

The spiritual question we must ask ourselves is,
"What will I do with what has been done to me?
Will I blame, shame, guilt myself?
Will I blame, shame, guilt others?
Will I recover? Will I heal?"
In the end, the hope is that the question will be,
"What has this done for me?"
instead of "What has this done to me?"

September 15

Some say by following your heart you will connect to
Mother Earth. The Elders say connect to Mother Earth,
and you will find your heart.

September 16

Harmony and Balance:
1. Always embrace what guides you.
2. Always release what no longer serves you.

September 17

All memories are medicine.
Some make it hard to let go of the past,
while others make it hard to move forward.
Often, we have to look at the memory to reveal
the lesson it takes for us to move on
and walk in a good way.

September 18

Letting go of those things that no longer
serve our life isn't the hard part;
the hard part is looking at the truth that it brings.

September 19

May all our actions be a reflection of our hope and faith.

WEST/
FALL

September 20

The fall medicine teaches us that
letting go can look beautiful.

September 21

We cannot find the truth
until it is the only thing we seek.

September 22

The Medicine Wheel teaches us
every season is a time grow.

September 23

Stillness is a super power.
Kindness is a super power.
Compassion is a super power.

September 24

The one who carries many secrets blinds himself.

September 25

The world transforms not by
misplaced judgements or opinions,
it begins with transformed personal growth
which includes forgiving the unforgivable
and loving the unlovable —
two of the most powerful choices
we must make every day.

September 26

The right to life includes all life.

September 27

The spiritual revolution will not look like violence
because the uprising is centered in love.
A seething and swelling of awareness and awakening,
vast in nature, every color of men and women standing
together, creating a whole.
One voice, one heart, one mind, one prayer, one people,
one Earth.

September 28

If our prayers do not include the next seven generations,
they are incomplete.

September 29

Those things in this world humanity thinks are wild,
like animals and flowers, are all relatives and medicine
to help guide us.
Only in absolute humility can we learn from them.
They are here to teach humanity how to act humanely.

September 30

One of the tragedies of life is living a life
without seeing the beauty we possess.

October 1

Like love, we hold on to gentleness by giving it away.

October 2

If we are not feeling the presence of our ancestors
walking with us, we are not
singing, dancing, or praying hard enough.

October 3

We are all searching for the light
until we decide we are the light.

October 4

Our best teacher is the love we offer.

October 5

Acceptance of the truth has nothing to do with
approval but everything to do with love.

October 6

To connect to the day, the season, and Creator,
we must take time to greet the great silence
in every new day.

October 7

Our spiritual choice happens when we find our power
and decide to walk with it or tiptoe around it.

October 8

Our prayers for others, especially between
men, nations, and religion, are not only vital for
humanity's survival but critical.

October 9

Our minds will find it hard to rest
until we have spoken our heart's truth.

October 10

Creator offers humanity endless opportunities daily. Are
we able to offer ourselves as many opportunities
as Creator does?

October 11

When we teach our children letting go can still be beautiful, we teach them the lessons of the Seasons and the Medicine Wheel.

October 12

Those who seek humility are heading toward greatness.

October 13

Imagination is a forgotten education,
because it teaches us endless possibilities.
Without it, it is only indoctrination.

October 14

Gratitude turns everything into abundance
and turns chaos into clarity.

October 15

Doubt has always been the beginning of
the road to faith.

October 16

If we are waiting for our next miracle,
let us remember our next breath is it.

October 17

Being Indigenous is based more on our relationship and honoring Mother Earth than it is blood quantum.

October 18

Like Earth, our spiritual growth is based on
our relationship to the light of the sun.

October 19

Without guidance from all four directions,
our emotions can take us on a journey we don't
want to go on.

October 20

Sometimes it only takes the next ceremony, song, prayer, or dance to change the direction of our lives.

October 21

Nothing is wasted in Mother Earth's economy.
When we offer what no longer serves us to Mother
Earth, Mother Earth is able to take this medicine and
turn it back into life.

October 22

Prayers are rewarded by patience.
And patience, in turn, rewards prayers.

October 23

When humility calls and we do not answer,
humiliation comes knocking.

October 24

Every time we go to ceremony,
we visit the heart of Creator.

October 25

Medicine Teaching:
We are taught to meet the moon and the sun
with the same respect.

October 26

Learning to love today helps us find a new tomorrow.

October 27

We have two choices:
1. Love = trust = evolve
2. Fear = worry = repeat

October 28

Mother Earth is so powerful because she decides patience and gentleness is the way to love.

October 29

The Medicine Wheel teaches us we may leave ceremony, but we should never allow ceremony to leave us.

October 30

Being amazing is always an option.

October 31

The ancestors remind us that higher awareness means always learning everything is a lesson.

November 1

Greed is a poor man's high.

November 2

When we disregard the odds against us,
the impossible becomes possible.

November 3

If the only lesson we have learned during our lifetime is how to love, that is enough.

November 4

Our Ancestors did not give us their prayers, love and courage so we could forget about them.
They gave us their prayers, love, and courage to help the next seven generations.

November 5

Our healing gives us insight on how to carry things
that once were immovable.

November 6

We are spiritually lacking when we want to be right before we want to listen.

November 7

We must understand the love that was here before the
sickness arrived on Turtle Island.
Our Indigenous songs, dances and ceremonies bring
back those memories to the people.

November 8

The tree is not ashamed that they were once a little nut
without roots, stem, or leaves. It accepts itself exactly
the way it is, in the exact moment it is in
without judgement or guilt.

November 9

Sweetgrass Medicine:
Let us intertwine our prayers to help us
stay strong together.

November 10

To walk in nature is to walk with Mother Earth.

November 11

The spiritual axiom is that beneath our human exterior
lies the stars of the universe.

November 12

It is not our job to have an opinion about what others think of us.

November 13

The one who understands the value of the unseen
has all the wealth they will ever need.

November 14

In order to love our Mother Earth, we have to be connected to Mother Earth. The old ones say we must sit with her, listen to her, sing with her, dance with her. Only then will we able to live in harmony with her. Until we do, we will only destroy her.

November 15

Those who have a difficult time listening
always have a difficult time healing.

November 16

Every rain drop carries the voices and wisdom of
our ancestors, offering life and hope.

November 17

The wind carries the prayers of our ancestors
from the beginning of time.

November 18

Our planet does not need saving as much it needs
humanity to awaken and save ourselves.
Only then will the planet be saved.

November 19

Until we listen to the heart of Mother Earth,
it will be hard to listen and understand our own heart.

November 20

For every breath, it is good to say "thank you" as often as
we can. For the air not only gives us life
but also gives us the breath of the powerful prayers
and wisdom of the ancient ones.

November 21

We should teach our children the ways our indigenous
parents were denied, the old ways that taught our
ancestors how to understand and live
in the ancient sacred agreements of harmony,
balance, rhythm, and flow.

November 22

We must learn to trust the medicine of the seasons.
Spring's renewal.
Summer's sun.
Fall's beauty of letting go in a good way and
winter of releasing what no longer serves life.

November 23

Mother Earth does not think any one nation or voice
is inferior to another.

November 24

Are you brave enough?

November 25

When our senses awaken and align with Mother Earth,
we begin to know a beautiful relationship with all life.

November 26

Which Path do we choose?
The colonial world wants to know who is right.
The Spirit world shows us what is right.

November 27

Those who have conquered their selfishness have
awakened to the Spirit.

November 28

The creatures of the night have a symphony all
their own, beginning with Grandmother Moon and
extending out in all directions.
We must listen to the darkness to heal.

November 29

The Medicine Wheel is not an assist,
it is a guide to build good relationships with all life.

November 30

Tears, like rain, are all holy water
and a gift from Creator.

December 1

Perspective right sizes our perspective

December 2

The Spirit name for the Medicine Wheel is humility.

December *3*

A healer's first lesson is Humility.
A healer's last lesson is humility.

December 4

If left untreated,
our wounds will speak louder than our voice ever could.

December 5

Healing, like ceremony, is not something we do
or a place we go. It is a way of life.

December 6

There is a stillness and patience inside each and every
one of us; it is not a remote place or a deep place.
It is found alongside the rhythm of Mother Nature
which we were born with.

December 7

The Medicine Wheel teaches there is as much wisdom to be learned in change as there is in stillness.

December 8

Winter teaches us that releasing what no longer serves us can be a beautiful ceremony.

December 9

Peace Medicine:
Peace is not the absence of conflict,
but learning to be peaceful in the face of it.

December 10

One of the hardest lessons to learn is to be gentle
in the face of mistreatment.

December 11

Great leaders are not forged in the fire of great stories or speaking wisdom, but by walking through challenges with great truths.

December 12

The prefect miracle is forgiving yourself.
The perfect time is now.

December 13

Helping others doesn't always mean we have all the answers; sometimes it means being willing to be present and simply listen.

December 14

The mind grows when it is open.
The heart grows when we share it.
The Earth heals when we offer both.

December 15

One word, one prayer, one offering can change the
world, beginning with yours.

December 16

A healer, like love, is a safe place when we are talking all sacred directions — physically, emotionally, mentally, and spiritually.

December 17

Listening is the original medicine.

December 18

Every inhale is a beautiful prayer.
Every exhale is beautiful prayer.
But left alone individually they cannot support life.
To understand and live a balanced life, we must keep
offering and receiving equally.

December 19

Remember, one day they will tell stories about us.
How that story is told is up to us.
What will your legacy be?

NORTH/
WINTER

December 20

The voices of the future come from
the prayers of our ancestors.

December 21

Trees look different when we can hear their voices.

December 22

The one true apology is changed behavior.

December 23

The reason we look to the stars at night is because
it is where we come from.
We are "Star People" and that is our home.

December 24

The old ones say to stay in prayer until you see the
beauty of Creator in everything.

December 25

The wise understand that sometimes speaking
your piece is more about not speaking at all.

December 26

Those who refuse to question their own spiritual path
will never understand any others.

December 27

Creator, teach me to see things I cannot see
with my eyes and learn to listen to those things
I cannot hear with my ears.

December 28

Like Mother Earth, the Spirits do not waste our time. They are always clear in their intentions. If we are unclear, it is us who are unfocused because we haven't yet learned how to listen.

December 29

We must honor those tears we have yet to offer.

December 30

The ancestor said, if you are alive, you are not only a survivor, you are a flame they could not extinguish.

December 31

We must always leave a place in our hearts
for the unimaginably wonderful and the
incomprehensibly beautiful.

January 1

Mother Earth had a dream once, and it looked exactly like the dreams of our ancestors.

January 2

The wise are very careful never to let knowledge
get in the way of wisdom.

January 3

Our personal peace, as well as humanity's, is based on our delicate balance and alignment, matching our insides to Mother Earth's outsides.

January 4

When we have come to a place where
we are honored to pray for those
who have wounded us,
we are in a beautiful place.

January 5

Having judgements before listening
guarantees we will not be able to hear.

January 6

The ones who offer their time to those
who are wounded give them a safe place land.
The ones who offer their ears to those
who are wounded give them wings to fly.

January 7

Those who understand the Spirit understand
they know very little about the Spirit.

January 8

Those who try suffer far less
than those who do not try at all.

January 9

Feel it, heal it, and release it.

January 10

The spoken word is the final result of our heartfelt
intention. The more pure our intentions,
the clearer and sweeter our words will be.

January 11

If we fall, starting over isn't a right, it is a privilege.

January 12

We don't always want to do the right thing, but doing the right thing is always right.

January 13

There is no logical end to prayer because there is no logical end to love. Only our species see illogical in logical. There is never a good reason to stop either. Stay in prayer, and you will stay in love.

January 14

As a species, one of our main problems is our inability to be alone with Mother Earth let alone build a sustainable relationship with her.

January 15

Praying for the sick to get well is good but praying for them to awaken is better. The awakened spirits understand the power of connection to all Spirits both seen and unseen.

January 16

We must be mindful;
what sounds like truth and awakening to the mind
may feel completely different to the heart.

January 17

Honoring all nations on Earth is not only honoring
two-legged nations but all nations,
from the four legged, standing, winged, mineral,
fish, creepy crawly, and slithery.

January 18

Our Elders say always carry your medicine with you
so your medicine may carry you.

January 19

Offering death to hate can be gentle and often looks like kindness, compassion and gentleness.

January 20

The Medicine Wheel teaches us every season we are to release the old and embrace the new.

January 21

There are no masters or gurus.
There are only those who want to remain asleep
and those who wish to awaken.

January 22

When we withhold forgiveness, we keep ourselves from enjoying the natural rhythm and flow of connectedness and alignment. When we begin to walk through the process of forgiveness, we enter into the realm of the Spirit and into that rhythm and flow.

January 23

I don't connect to Mother Earth using my mind.
I connect to Mother Earth with my heart.

January 24

Winter is a time for self-reflection, to look at what no longer serves us and our community.

January 25

The beauty and love we possess is a gift from our
ancestors. We are only a steward of this beauty and love,
and we must offer this to our future generations.

January 26

Creator, please let me hear what I cannot see.
Creator, please let me see what I cannot hear.

January 27

Humanity is in dire need of powerful spiritual allies like the tree nation, the four legged, the fish people, creepy crawlies nations, the winged, and all other life.

January 28

It is always good to ask in prayer if we are in alignment with the natural rhythm and flow of the seasons.

January 29

The feathers and the moccasins do not make the Indian.
It is the love in their heart.

January 30

The extinction of various species on Earth represents
the extinction of human awareness that
we are a part of Earth.

January 31

By avoiding our own truth, we place ourselves in a position where we will have a difficult time seeing, hearing, or understanding anyone else's.

February 1

The biggest secret of the dark is that to be effective,
it knows it needs the light.
The biggest secret of the light is that to be effective,
it knows it needs the dark.

February 2

Praying for and thanking the ancestors of all other
nations, the four legged, standing, winged, mineral, fish,
creepy crawly, and slithery is another beautiful
and essential way of connecting to
Mother Earth and the Spirit.

February 3

In Indigenous circles, it is our belief that
if our prayers do not include future generations
then our prayers are incomplete.

February 4

Wealth is our ability to love. Period.

February 5

In the days, weeks, and months leading up to the next season, it is time for us to set the prayerful intention for our growth for the next season.

February 6

Winter Medicine:
A time of reflection and action.
We must connect in ceremony and prayer to our
enemies within, to retrieve those things that no longer
serve life so we can offer those things to
the light of the new spring.

February 7

Spirit tells us, in one season there are many days but
Spirit also tells us we can experience many seasons
in one day.

February 8

Sometimes when walking the Red Road, we may feel like a fraud, especially if we come from another religion, spiritual path, or direction. However, the Spirit only sees self-deception in those walking a path that doesn't honor them or in one that doesn't honor all others.

February 9

Humility protects us from ourselves.

February 10

Our age means little to the season or Spirit. Both are only interested in our graceful growth and awakening.

February 11

If you choose to be anything, choose to be Grateful.

February 12

Maturity is walking through pain, knowing healing and
health are on the other side.
Immaturity is choosing not to walk through pain,
knowing healing and health are on the other side.

February 13

The old ones always say to begin the day with prayers of gratitude and end the day with prayers of thanks.

February 14

Our prayers give us a sacred window to listen to our
ancestors who have gone before us.

February 15

We must listen to the sacred elements of each season
to truly understand the gifts from Creator.

February 16

Winter doesn't have to decide if it is winter or not.
It just is.

February 17

As long as loving Mother Earth is an option in our mind instead of a priority in our heart, we will continue to struggle with relations in all parts of our lives.

February 18

The smallest steps may be insignificant but
let us remember the nut that existed before the tree
started. Beautiful things sometime start
very small and insignificant.

February 19

In Sweatlodge ceremony, sometimes you choose the warrior round. But in life, sometimes the warrior round chooses you.

February 20

The Medicine Wheel and the seasons teach us we are constantly transforming. Into what is entirely up to us.

February 21

Forgiveness:
Our most powerful weapon is prayers of love and light
for those who have harmed us.
Our abusers may not hear but
our hearts and Creator will.

February 22

In prayer, if we do not introduce our ancestors when we introduce ourselves, our introduction is incomplete.

February 23

The war and chaos humanity feels on the collective inside is represented in the world we created on the collective outside.

February 24

The Medicine Wheel says we walk and live many lives
in this one life.

February 25

Pretending our Mother Earth is okay is not okay.

February 26

The four seasons tell us nothing ever dies,
it all transforms into something else.

February 27

Sad, depressed, and lonely?
Start with what our ancestors never stopped doing:
singing, dancing, and ceremony.

February 28

The truth is a small price to pay but sometimes
a huge mountain to climb.

February 29

Paradise, that place humanity is looking for,
begins within you.

March 1

Humanity must understand it takes great humility to honor, love, and pray with and for those Nations on Mother Earth that do not speak, look, or talk like us, like the four legged, standing, winged, mineral, fish, creepy crawly, slithery. Our connection begins here.

March 2

When we've come to a place where we are honored to pray for those who have wounded us, we are in a beautiful ceremony of light and love.

March 3

Humility is humanity's most forgotten ceremony.

March 4

The Great Spirit offers us all the seasons
to teach us how to grow, learn, and change
with grace and absolute beauty.

March 5

The Medicine Wheel teaches that the Physical and the
Spiritual always mirror each other.
To awaken, we must physically align ourselves with
those who are spiritually awake.

March 6

Showing love, compassion, and respect for others speaks
volumes about the love, compassion, and respect
we carry for ourselves.

March 7

Those who choose to be grateful choose life.

March 8

Indigenous language is the voice of our ancestors.
To truly understand our cultural journey, others have
acquainted themselves with our language.

Happy Birthday
lovely

♡
Ⓧ

March 9

Mother Earth is our natural law.
As Indigenous people, we have always known
she is the only true authority over our lands.

March 10

As we approach spring, we must remember not to pick up those things we just let go of that no longer serve our highest good.

March 11

The birthplace of courage is humility.
The birthplace of humility is truth.
The birthplace of truth is courage.

March 12

Winter medicine is reflection and
a time for self-reflection.

March 13

If done correctly,
our listening should interrupt our talking.

March 14

Those who connect and maintain a connection to
Spirit and Mother Earth will lead a very different life
than those who do not.

March 15

Grief doesn't care if it is healthy or not.
We can grieve for something good or something
unhealthy. What matters most is that we find the
courage to move through it.

March 16

Let us make good relations with beautiful allies such as the four seasons, Friends of the Spirit who give medicine in a good and gentle way.

March 17

We are Indigenous because we are Earth
not because we walk on her.

March 18

When we clean up Mother Earth,
the unseen forces always see and reciprocate.

March 19

There is life, a beautiful life, after forgiving the
unforgivable and loving the unlovable.

Glossary of Terms

1. Indigenous: Refers to those of ancestral lineage from North, Central and South America.

2. Great Spirit: A general indigenous term referring to the mighty power of God that flows through all life. The Creator of all life. A life force that is both seen and unseen, male and female.

3. Red Road: Indigenous spiritual path.

4. Ceremony: A particular spiritual event but could also be considered our life's spiritual walk.

5. All our relations: a specific Indigenous Spiritual term usually used at the end of our prayer, identifying and in reference to Mother Earth and all who reside on her. All life, plant nations, animals, fish people, winged nations, creepy crawlers, slithery nations, insect nations, fire, water, and air.

6. Smudge: An act of spiritual cleansing or clearing negative energies, usually by a sacred smoke from sage, cedar, sweetgrass, or tobacco.

7. Prayer: A spiritual request for wisdom, healing, answers, or guidance.

8. Offering(s): Sacred items are given so our prayers will be heard, usually in the form of tobacco or any

number of other sacred plant medicines and up to and including ourselves. Always given with sacred intent and purpose.

9. Four sacred directions: East, South, West and North.

10. Turtle Island: North America, a name Indigenous use when referring to the Northern Hemisphere.

11. Mother Earth: Our sacred Mother.

12. Ancestor(s): Our past relations, or relatives, those both in physical and spiritual realms.

13. Hollow Bone: A term coined by our ancestors about being a conduit for the Great Spirit to work and flow through us, becoming a vessel of love, light, healing, and life.

14. Walking in a good way: Our sacred journey through life walking with and for the Great Spirit.

15. Sweat lodge: A sacred prayer and healing ceremony where we enter into the womb of Mother Earth.

16. Wound(s): We are speaking in spiritual terms, referring to unhealed emotional hurts. Grief, mourning, and childhood trauma.

17. Love: In spiritual realms, love has nothing to do with physical contact. It means I want everything good for you, but I want nothing from you.

18. Medicine: In spiritual realms, a thought or idea can be considered medicine. Not just the physical. For example, Love is powerful medicine, it comes in many forms. A thought, a prayer, flowers, a hug. Compassion. Kindness.

19. Medicine Wheel: Also referred to as the sacred hoop, this is a physical reflection of our spiritual self. It embodies the health and the cycles of life that we live in. This aligns our spiritual life force with those around us, including Mother Earth.

20. Sacred center: That special and specific place of balance, love, and nurturing within us. The God light or the eternal flame within.

21. Standing nations: Trees and plants.

22. Spiritual Innocence: State of unknowing; pure, like a baby.

About the Author

Wayne William Snellgrove, a Saulteaux Indian, was born on Fishing Lake First Nation Reserve in Saskatchewan. He is a modern-day genocide survivor of the Canadian government's policy of assimilation known as The 60s Scoop, a two-time USA National swimming champion and a USA Swimming National Team member. He divides his time between the Canadian province of Saskatchewan and the state of Ohio in the U.S.

Printed in the USA
CPSIA information can be obtained
at www.ICGtesting.com
LVHW020055210624
783564LV00014B/970

9 781948 979511